THE FINANCIAL IDENTITY SHIFT

REBUILD WHO YOU BELIEVE YOU ARE WITH MONEY

Author/Editor: Rev. Darryl Bass

Printed in the United States

Electronic ISBN: 978-1-972115-04-6 (EPUB)
                  978-1-972115-30-5 (Kindle)
Paperback ISBN: 978-1-972115-03-9
Hardcover ISBN: 978-1-972115-05-3

The Library of Congress Control Number: 2026906576

Disclaimer

The information contained in this book is for educational and informational purposes only. It is not intended as financial, legal, tax, medical, psychological, or professional advice. The author and publisher make no guarantees regarding the results that may be obtained from the use of this material.

All examples provided are illustrative and are not intended to represent or guarantee that any individual will achieve similar results. Personal growth, financial improvement, and life progression outcomes depend on individual effort, discipline, decisions, and circumstances.

Readers are encouraged to seek qualified professional advice regarding financial planning, legal matters, mental health, or other specialized areas before making decisions based on the information provided in this book.

The author and publisher disclaim any liability for any loss, risk, or damages, direct or indirect, that may arise from the use or application of the information contained herein.

By reading this book, you acknowledge that you are responsible for your own decisions, actions, and results.

Details in these stories and anecdotes have been changed to protect the identities of the person(s) involved.

Contents

Acknowledgment

I thank God, who is the source of wisdom, identity, and every breakthrough that takes root in the heart. Without His guidance, revelation, and presence, none of this would have formed or flowed.

To my family — thank you for your love, honesty, patience, and belief in me. You are the reason legacy matters. You are my "why."

To those I have walked with, coached, taught, prayed for, encouraged, and watched grow — thank you for trusting me to speak into your journey. Your transformation has shaped mine. Your healing has expanded my understanding. Your victories have strengthened my faith.

To my mentors, spiritual leaders, and every person who has ever poured into me — thank you for sharpening me, challenging me, and preparing me to stand in this assignment.

And to the reader — thank you for your **yes.**
Thank you for showing up for yourself.
Thank you for being willing to heal, unlearn, and rebuild.
Your courage is the beginning of generational change.

We are building legacy — together.

Dedication

This book is dedicated to every person who has ever felt overlooked, underestimated, or unprepared when it came to money.

To those who were taught to **survive**, but never shown how to **build**.

To those who worked hard, prayed hard, and hoped hard — yet never experienced the peace and confidence they deserved.

This is for you.

For the ones who decided that the cycle ends here.
For the ones who are rising.
For the ones who are becoming.

May you rediscover who you truly are —
and walk boldly into the identity, abundance, and legacy that belongs to you.

Foreword

Money affects every part of our lives — our peace, our decisions, our relationships, our self-image, and our future. But most of us were handed financial beliefs before we ever had the chance to choose our own.

We inherited:

- Patterns
- Fears
- Habits
- Struggles
- Silence
- Survival thinking

Not because our families failed —
but because **they were surviving a world they were never prepared for.**

This book is not about blame.
It is about **awareness, healing, and identity reconstruction.**

You are not here by coincidence.
You are here because something in you knows:

"There is more to my life than this."

Not more struggle.
Not more stress.
Not more pretending everything is okay.

More peace.
More clarity.

More wisdom.
More purpose.
More legacy.

This book will not only teach you how to handle money differently —
It will teach you how to **be someone different with money.**

Read slowly.
Reflect deeply.
Allow your identity to shift from the inside out.

Your life will not be the same.

Introduction — You Cannot Outgrow the Identity You Haven't Rebuilt

Most people believe financial breakthrough happens when you:

- Make more money
- Start a business
- Get a promotion
- Repair credit
- Pay off debt

But **none of these things will last** if your identity does not change.

Because **your financial life will always return to the level of your financial self-image.**

If deep down, you still believe:

- "I always end up behind…"
- "Money is stressful…"
- "People like me don't get ahead…"
- "I don't deserve more…"

Then no matter how much progress you make externally — your internal identity will pull you back into the familiar.

This is why people:

- Get raises but still feel broke
- Pay off debt but end up back in it
- Start saving but drain their accounts under pressure
- Make more money but never feel secure

Change that doesn't happen in identity cannot be sustained.

This book is an invitation to:

- Rebuild your identity
- Break inherited financial patterns
- Heal the emotional side of money
- Develop a peaceful and structured relationship with finances
- Step into purpose-driven increase
- And create legacy for those who will come after you

This is not about money.

This is about **who you are becoming.**

The Financial Identity Shift begins now.

SECTION I: Identity Before Income

Chapter One: Who Told You That You Were Broke?

Your first identity was formed long before you could speak.
Before you could count.
Before you knew what a bill, a paycheck, or a credit score even was.

You learned money through:

- Tone of voice
- Reactions to crises
- Emotional climate
- Offhand comments
- Household habits

Maybe you heard:

- "We don't have it."
- "Money is hard."
- "People like us don't get ahead."
- "Rich people are greedy."
- "Just pray and hope things work out."

These statements didn't just inform you...
They **shaped you.**

You didn't just inherit behaviors.
You inherited a **financial identity.**

And often that identity was built on:

- Survival, not abundance
- Hustling, not structure

- Making it, not multiplying it
- Hope, not systems
- Emotional coping, not stewardship

Identity is programmed through experience and environment.
Which means identity can be **reprogrammed through awareness and alignment.**

This chapter awakens that awareness.

Reflection Moment

Ask yourself:

- What did I learn *about money* growing up?
- What did I learn *about myself* financially growing up?
- Whose financial identity am I currently living out?

Your breakthrough begins where your honesty begins.

Identity Declaration

I release every identity that was formed from lack, fear, shame, and survival. I am being rebuilt into wisdom, stewardship, discipline, and abundance. My past does not define my financial future. I am becoming someone new.

Chapter Two: The Silent Agreements That Shape Your Finances

There are things people *say* about money, and then there are the things they **believe** about money—often silently, unconsciously, without ever speaking them aloud.

These silent agreements run your financial life more than budgets or paychecks ever could.

A **silent agreement** is:

- A belief you didn't choose
- A conclusion you didn't examine
- A financial identity you adopted without question

They are formed in:

- Childhood conversations
- Cultural norms
- Family traditions
- Church teachings
- Trauma
- Disappointment
- Comparison
- Shame

They program identity by shaping your *internal definition* of what is normal, possible, allowed, or expected for you.

Examples of Silent Agreements

You may have formed silent agreements like:

- "I have to struggle to prove I'm strong."
- "If I earn more, people will expect too much from me."
- "Money creates conflict, so I'll avoid it."
- "It's safer to have just enough than to aim for more."
- "If I succeed financially, I'll be alone."
- "We don't talk about money in this family."
- "God wants me humble, not prosperous."

Silent agreements don't sound loud.
They operate like background apps draining your battery without you noticing.

How Silent Agreements Show Up in Daily Life

You can recognize a silent agreement by observing your consistent patterns:

- Do you undercharge even though you serve at a high level?
- Do you give more than you financially have because you fear appearing selfish?
- Do you get uncomfortable when money starts increasing?
- Do you feel guilt when you buy something for yourself?
- Do you avoid budgeting because seeing the reality feels overwhelming?

That's not personality.
That's not "just how you are."

That is **identity coding.**

And identity can be rewritten.

The Emotional Origins of Money Decisions

Money decisions are rarely about math.
They are about:

- Safety
- Worthiness
- Identity
- Approval
- Fear of loss
- Fear of rejection
- Fear of responsibility

For example:

- Overspending may be rooted in a desire to feel valued or seen.
- Under-earning may be tied to feeling undeserving of more.
- Avoidance may be a trauma response to chaos or control in childhood.
- Giving away too much may be tied to needing to be loved.

Financial healing requires emotional honesty.

Reflection Exercise: Identify the Silent Agreement

Complete this sentence:

"Part of me believes that if I become financially strong,

_____."

Write without thinking.
Let the truth rise.

Now complete:

"The first time I learned to fear money was when

_____."

That memory holds the key.

Breaking the Agreement

A silent agreement can be replaced with a **spoken identity** backed by conscious alignment.

Speak this:

I am allowed to prosper without apology.
I am safe to increase.
I do not have to choose between being spiritual and being financially wise.
I am trusted by God to steward increase well.
My identity is shifting to match the future God prepared for me.

Identity Declaration

I break every silent agreement that has tied me to lack, fear, guilt, or limitation. I step into a renewed identity where wealth is an expression of wisdom, stewardship, peace, and divine assignment. I am worthy of abundance because I am worthy of purpose.

Chapter Three: The Misalignment Between Who You Are and How You Handle Money

Most people are not financially stuck because they lack intelligence, discipline, or opportunity.
They are stuck because **their financial practices do not match who they desire to become.**

This is identity misalignment.

Think of it like this:
If your mind sees you as someone who "just gets by," then even if you start making more, your spending, saving, and stewardship will shift to return you to the identity you believe is yours.

This is why lottery winners go broke.
Why promotions don't fix financial stress.
Why new income streams still collapse into old cycles.

Income without identity simply magnifies dysfunction.

The Three Layers of Financial Alignment

To fully step into the Financial Identity Shift, you must align:

Layer	Focus	Questions to Ask Yourself
Belief (Who I believe I am)	Identity	*Do I see myself as someone who manages money well and honors God in stewardship?*
Behavior (What I repeatedly do)	Habits	*Do my daily decisions reflect the level of wisdom and discipline I desire?*

Layer	Focus	Questions to Ask Yourself
Structure (The systems I use)	Strategy	*Do I have processes that support consistency, peace, and growth?*

If even one layer is misaligned, progress becomes temporary.

Identity → Behavior → Structure → Fruit

Most people try to change the *fruit* (debt, credit, income). But the transformation begins at the *root*.

Signs of Misalignment

You are most likely experiencing identity misalignment if:

- You know what to do, but don't do it consistently.
- You feel anxious when finances improve.
- You're uncomfortable discussing money directly.
- You avoid looking at bank statements until it's "necessary."
- You delay decisions hoping the situation changes by itself.
- You give beyond your ability because "you don't want to be selfish."
- You feel guilt when money comes to you easily.

These are not character flaws.
They are **identity conflicts**.

Your *current identity* is trying to protect what's familiar.
Your *future identity* is trying to be born.

This is the moment of shift.

The Identity Alignment Practice

This practice begins the process of financial identity reconstruction:

1. **Name Your Current Money Identity**
   Examples:
   - The Survivor
   - The Saver
   - The Giver Who Can't Say No
   - The Hustler
   - The Avoider
   - The Fixer
   - The "I'll Figure It Out Later"
2. **Name Your Becoming Identity**
   Examples:
   - The Strategic Steward
   - The Investor
   - The Builder
   - The Legacy Maker
   - The Generational Breaker
3. **Create One Daily Behavior That Matches the Identity You Are Becoming**
   Examples:
   - Checking your accounts daily without fear.
   - Setting a weekly "money appointment."
   - Saying "not right now" to purchases without emotional guilt.
   - Tracking spending for awareness, not shame.
   - Giving from overflow, not obligation.

Identity shifts through repeated alignment, not through force.

Reflection Questions

- Which identity am I currently living from?
- Which identity do I desire to embody moving forward?
- What is *one small, daily habit* I can commit to that aligns me with who I am becoming?

Write it.
Speak it.
Walk it.

Identity Declaration

I am no longer living from the identity of survival, lack, fear, or unworthiness. I embody the identity of a wise steward, a builder of legacy, a vessel of increase. My behaviors are aligning with wisdom, order, and stewardship. I am stepping into who I was always meant to be.

SECTION II: The Inner Reconstruction

Chapter Four: You Cannot Build Wealth on a Wounded Identity

If the part of you that handles money is still hurting, afraid, ashamed, or unhealed, no amount of financial knowledge will change your life.

You can learn:

- How to budget
- How to invest
- How to repair credit
- How to increase your income

…but if your **identity is wounded**, your decisions will always circle back to pain.

Because **money does not reveal who you want to be— money exposes who you currently are.**

A wounded identity with money may show up as:

- Spending to feel valuable
- Giving to feel worthy
- Avoiding finances to escape stress
- Working nonstop to prove something
- Undercharging because you don't believe your value
- Sabotaging progress because success feels unfamiliar

Money becomes emotional long before it ever becomes mathematical.

You are not just shifting finances.
You are healing the person inside of you who was never taught safety around money.

The Identity Wound Behind Every Financial Struggle

There are three primary identity wounds that shape financial behavior:

Identity Wound	Core Emotion	Financial Pattern
Unworthiness	"I don't deserve more."	Under-earning, over-giving, self-sabotage
Fear of Responsibility	"What if I mess it up?"	Avoidance, procrastination, dependency
Fear of Judgment	"What will people think?"	Overspending, image-based purchases, secrecy

Each wound was formed through lived experience—not weakness.

It may have come from:

- Growing up watching instability
- Being shamed for asking for help
- Witnessing money cause conflict
- Being told to "be humble" but never taught stewardship
- Having to become "the strong one" too early
- Feeling overlooked or undervalued
- Surviving rather than growing

Your wound has a history.
But it does not need a future.

Healing Comes Through Identity Restoration

This is not about becoming someone new.
It is about becoming who you **were before life taught you to fear money.**

You were born worthy.
You were born with purpose.
You were born with capacity.
You were born with inheritance—spiritually, emotionally, financially.

Life didn't break your purpose.
It only buried it.

This chapter is about **digging you out.**

The Restoration Process (The 3 R's)

1. **Reveal**
   Name the wound without shame.
   "I am not weak—I am waking up."
2. **Release**
   Let go of the identity that was built in survival.
   You are allowed to stop fighting battles that no longer exist.
3. **Rebuild**
   Adopt practices that reinforce who you are becoming.
   This is where discipline becomes devotion—not punishment.

Healing Work: The Money Memory Reset

Write down a financial memory that shaped your identity.

Then answer:

- How old was I in that moment?
- What did I *decide about myself* because of that moment?
- Is that decision still serving me today?

Then say out loud:

I release the version of me that had to survive that season.
I honor them, but I am not them anymore.
I am safe to grow.
I am safe to increase.
I am safe to win.

Repeat slowly.
Let it sink.

Identity Declaration

I am not building wealth from woundedness.
I am building wealth from wisdom, peace, clarity, and divine identity.
I am worthy of abundance.
I am trustworthy with increase.
I am safe to step into overflow.
I am becoming the builder, the steward, the leader, the generational shifter I was always meant to be.

Chapter Five: Rewriting Your Financial Self-Image

You will never consistently rise above the way you *see yourself* financially.

Your financial life will always reflect your **self-image** — not your goals, not your desires, not your dreams — your internal identity.

Self-image answers the question:

"Who am I when it comes to money?"

For many, the answer has been shaped by:

- Past mistakes
- Seasons of survival
- Family patterns
- Moments of embarrassment
- Breakdowns you had to silently recover from

So when you try to elevate financially...
Your current self-image may resist.

Not because you can't grow.
Not because God is withholding anything.
But because **identity always returns to familiarity.**

To shift your finances, you must **rewrite your internal definition of who you are with money.**

What Is the Financial Self-Image?

Your financial self-image is the internal story you believe about:

- What is possible for you
- What is "normal" for you
- What you are allowed to have
- What you are capable of managing
- What you are worthy of receiving

If you believe:

- "I always figure it out eventually," then you live in crisis-and-recovery cycles.
- "I'm not a money person," then you avoid structure.
- "Money stresses me out," then you disconnect from stewardship.
- "Every time I get ahead, something happens," then your life will obey that expectation.

These are not personality traits.
They are identity scripts that must be rewritten.

Rewriting Begins with Re-Seeing

To shift your financial identity, you must start seeing yourself as:

- Capable
- Confident
- Calm around money
- Trusted by God
- Consistent
- Discerning
- Worthy of overflow

Not "someday."
Now.

Because your life can only manifest what your identity supports.

You don't wait to have money to become wise.
You become wise so the money has somewhere safe to land.

The Financial Self-Image Exercise

Step 1: Define Your Old Identity

Write the identity that has been running your finances:

Examples:

- "I'm always behind."
- "I'm just trying to survive."
- "I'm doing my best but can't get ahead."

Step 2: Define Your New Identity

Write who you are becoming:

Examples:

- "I am a faithful steward."
- "I am disciplined and intentional."
- "I manage money with clarity and peace."

Step 3: Anchor the Identity Daily

Not with hype.
With habits.

Because consistency builds identity.

Choose one of these daily alignment actions:

Action	Identity Reinforced
Check your accounts daily	"I face money without fear."
Track spending weekly	"I am intentional and aware."
Create a weekly money appointment	"I lead my financial life."
Pay yourself first	"I deserve stability and growth."
Say "not yet" without guilt	"My future matters to me."

Small steps.
Done daily.
Shift identity faster than big dramatic changes.

Why This Works

Your brain believes what you do repeatedly.
So identity is not changed by motivation — it's changed by **rhythm.**

Your new identity isn't something you "try on."
It's something you **practice until it becomes your default.**

Identity Declaration

I see myself differently now.
I handle money with clarity, confidence, and wisdom.
I am not a struggler, hustler, survivor, or reactor.
I am a builder, I am a steward.
I am a creator of legacy.
I walk in my financial identity with consistency and peace.

Chapter Six: Healing Emotional Spending & Rebuilding Financial Capacity

You do not spend money only for *needs*.
You spend money for:

- Comfort
- Validation
- Escape
- Relief
- Identity
- Belonging
- Celebration
- Avoidance
- Security
- Expression

Money has always been emotional before it is mathematical.

This is why someone can say *"I know better"* and still:

- Buy what they can't afford
- Give beyond their ability
- Hide purchases
- Shop to soothe stress
- Spend to feel worthy

Emotional spending is not irresponsibility — it is self-soothing.
It is the heart trying to heal with the wrong tool.

But hear this with compassion and truth:

What your heart needs cannot be purchased.
It must be rebuilt.

And you are rebuilding now.

The Emotional Root Behind Overspending

Most emotional spending is linked to one of three internal states:

Emotional Root	What It Feels Like	How It Shows Up in Spending
Lack of Worthiness	"I need to feel valuable."	Buying to feel seen, polished, respected
Emotional Exhaustion	"I need relief."	Impulse spending, food delivery, convenience splurges
Identity Insecurity	"I need to look okay."	Status-based purchases, image-driven spending

The spending is the *symptom*.
The identity wound is the *cause*.

We heal the wound — and the spending changes on its own.

Step One: Pause the Pattern (Without Shame)

Shame does not create change — shame creates hiding.

We interrupt emotional spending with **awareness**, not punishment.

Before spending, ask:

"What do I actually need right now?"

Sometimes the answer is:

- Rest
- Reassurance
- Encouragement
- Support
- Connection
- Permission to slow down
- Prayer
- Reflection
- Silence

Not the purchase.

Step Two: Replace Emotional Spending with Emotional Regulation

Here are emotional replacements that restore peace:

Emotion	Need	Healthy Replacements
Overwhelmed	Relief	Step outside. Breathe. Drink water. Reset.
Lonely	Connection	Call someone who nourishes you.

Emotion	Need	Healthy Replacements
Sad	Comfort	Put on worship. Journal. Pray honestly.
Insecure	Identity	Speak your identity declaration out loud.
Bored	Stimulation	Create something. Move your body. Learn.

The goal is not to suppress emotion.
The goal is to care for the heart **without costing the future.**

Step Three: Rebuild Capacity (The Practical Side)

Once the emotional leaks are addressed, you now have the internal stability to build and hold financial capacity.

Financial Capacity = The ability to hold, manage, and sustain increase.

To build capacity, we begin with:

1. Margin

Margin is space — emotional and financial.

Start with:

- A small $50–$100 **buffer account**
- No pressure, no shame, no perfection
- Just proof to your brain: *"I can hold money."*

2. Structure

Create one weekly "Money Appointment" with yourself:

- 15–30 minutes
- Same day, same time
- Check accounts, update budget, plan week

This consistency builds identity and peace.

3. Boundaries

Say:

"Not now, but soon."

Not from lack — from **vision.**

Boundaries protect your future self.

Reflection Exercise

Answer slowly:

1. When I spend emotionally, what am I actually needing?
2. What emotional replacement will I use moving forward?
3. What day and time will I set for my weekly money appointment?

Write it.
Speak it.
Commit to it.

Identity Declaration

I no longer use money to heal what only peace can restore.
I honor my emotions without sabotaging my future.
I am learning to hold money with patience, clarity, and wisdom.
I am safe to build capacity.
I am becoming trustworthy with abundance.

Chapter Seven: The Steward's System:

A Financial Structure That Supports

Peace, Growth, and Overflow

Money is not multiplied through emotion — it is multiplied through order.

God is a God of **structure.**
Creation itself was formed in **sequence, layers, and alignment.**
When your finances align with structure, peace enters your life.

When you gain structure, you no longer:

- Chase bills
- React to emergencies
- Live from emotional highs and lows
- Feel like money is "random" or unpredictable

Structure creates stability.
Stability creates confidence.
Confidence creates consistency.
Consistency creates increase.

We are not just building wealth —
We are building the *container* that can hold wealth.

The Purpose of a Stewardship System

This system is not about restriction.
It is about **relationship** — your relationship with money.

Structure says:

"I honor what God has placed in my hands.
I am trustworthy with increase.
I make decisions from identity, not emotion."

This system simplifies finances so your mind can rest and
your future can grow.

The Three-Account Stewardship System

We use **three accounts** — not one — because each account
has a job.

Account	Purpose	Identity Message
Account #1: Life Operations	Daily living expenses	"I manage my life with clarity and peace."
Account #2: The Stewardship Vault	Savings + Future Goals + Margin	"I am capable of holding money."
Account #3: Purpose & Assignment Giving	Tithing, offerings, generosity	"My increase is connected to Kingdom assignment."

This structure aligns finances with:

- **Wisdom**
- **Discipline**
- **Spiritual identity**
- **Emotional maturity**
- **Long-term stewardship**

Step-by-Step Setup Instructions

1. Open Three Separate Checking/Savings Accounts

- One account for **operating expenses**
- One **savings** account (Vault)
- One **giving** account

You can use:

- Your current bank
- Or open additional free accounts at online banks like Capital One 360, Ally, Chime, or Credit Union accounts

The bank does not matter — the identity assignment does.

2. Begin Allocating Income Using the 70/20/10 Identity Alignment Formula

This is NOT a rule — it is a starting rhythm.

Category	Percentage	Purpose
70% → **Life Operations**	Bills, groceries, transportation, household needs	
20% → **Stewardship Vault**	Savings, emergency fund, future purchases	
10% → **Giving**	Tithes, offerings, charitable support	

If 70/20/10 is too tight right now, start with:

90/5/5, then grow into **80/10/10**, then up to 70/20/10.

The goal is not perfection —
The goal is **progress into alignment.**

3. Automate the Transfers

The system works best when:

- Your income is deposited into your **Life Operations Account**
- And **automatic transfers** send money to your Vault and Giving accounts **every payday**

Automation removes:

- Emotional decision-making
- Guilt
- Forgetting
- Overspending

Your identity aligns through **consistency without willpower battles.**

4. Schedule Your Weekly "Money Appointment"

Once per week — same day, same time:

30 minutes.
No rushing.
No shame.
No panic.

During this time:

- Review account balances
- Confirm upcoming bills
- Check your spending rhythm
- Celebrate where you stayed aligned

This is not bookkeeping.
This is **identity strengthening.**

This appointment says:

"I lead my finances.
My finances do not lead me."

Why This System Creates Peace

Because you no longer:

- Wonder where your money went
- Spend from guilt or impulse
- Wait until emergencies to face reality

You experience peace because:

- Your money has direction
- Your decisions match your identity
- Your finances reflect order and intentionality

This is stewardship.
This is maturity.
This is spiritual alignment made practical.

Identity Declaration

I honor what God has given me.
I am trusted with increase.
I manage money with clarity, peace, and wisdom.
My finances are in divine order.
I am building a future with stability and purpose.
I am becoming the steward Heaven can trust with more.

Chapter Eight: Becoming the Builder

Increasing Income Through Purpose, Strategy, and Assignment

Financial identity is not just about healing.
It is about **building.**

Because at some point, the healed version of you must rise and say:

"Now I am ready to create."

Money does not multiply by accident.
Increase is not random.
Wealth is not something we wait for — it is something we **build with intention.**

And to build, you must know:

1. **Who you are,**
2. **Why you are here,**
3. **What you are called to create,**
4. **And who you are assigned to impact.**

You are not here to chase income.
You are here to produce **value that transforms lives** — and income flows to value.

Purpose First. Strategy Second. Income Third.

The world trains people to chase money.

But Kingdom order is:

1. **Identity** → Who I am
2. **Purpose** → Why I exist
3. **Assignment** → Who I am sent to
4. **Value** → What I create to serve them
5. **Income** → The exchange that flows back to me

When identity is aligned,
When purpose is rooted,
When assignment is clear,

Money comes as a byproduct — not a pursuit.

The Calling That Produces Income

You have **natural value** embedded in you.

Your calling is not something you invent.
It is something you *remember* — something that has always been there.

Ask yourself:

- What do I do naturally that others struggle to do?
- What comes easily to me that others pay for?
- What do people always ask me for guidance on?
- What energizes me instead of draining me?
- What have I survived that I can now help others overcome?

Your **anointing reveals your assignment.**

Your **assignment reveals your audience.**

Your **audience reveals your income model.**

The 4 Assignment Archetypes

Every person falls into at least one:

Archetype	Purpose Expression	Primary Income Path
Teacher	Shares knowledge and wisdom	Courses, coaching, speaking, books
Builder	Creates systems, structures, and processes	Business, operations consulting, management
Healer	Helps restore emotional, spiritual, or mental wellness	Counseling, ministry, wellness, coaching
Creator	Brings beauty, meaning, and experience into the world	Art, media, music, design, branding

Your assignment is the intersection of all four questions:

(1) What I can do
(2) What I enjoy doing
(3) What helps someone else
(4) And what people will exchange value for

This is where income becomes *purpose-led*.

The Strategy That Multiplies Income

Once identity and assignment are aligned, we build income through **The Income Expansion Ladder:**

Level	Focus	Outcome
1. Solve One Problem	Identify one clear result you can deliver	Clarity & demand
2. Serve One Audience	Speak to one type of person consistently	Deep connection
3. Create One Offer	A simple, results-based service or program	Income stability
4. Scale One System	Automate, document, and streamline	Capacity for growth

You don't start with **multiple income streams**.
You start with **one well-built stream** that flows consistently.

Then—and only then—do you multiply.

Practical Action: Build Your Income Assignment Statement

Complete this sentence:

I help (who) overcome/achieve (what), by providing (how), so they can (transformation/result).

Example:

I help working families break the paycheck-to-paycheck cycle by teaching practical financial alignment, so they can build stability, dignity, and generational wealth.

This becomes:

- Your brand message
- Your offer clarity
- Your marketing direction

- Your identity anchor

Identity Declaration

I am called to build.
I am called to increase.
I do not chase money; I produce value.
I serve with clarity, purpose, and excellence.
I am trusted to create wealth that honors God and impacts generations.
I walk boldly in my assignment.

SECTION III: Becoming the

Steward God Intended

Chapter Nine: The Discipline of the Builder

You cannot pray for a future you are not willing to prepare for.

Many people want overflow, increase, and financial freedom—but do not yet carry the **discipline, consistency, or structure** required to sustain it.

Increase is not only a blessing.
Increase is **responsibility.**

And God will never send increase into a life that does not have the capacity to *hold* it.

Because God does not waste increase.

If there is no structure—money slips away.
If there is no discipline—goals never solidify into progress.
If there is no accountability—identity collapses under pressure.
If there is no maturity—financial blessings become financial burdens.

This is not punishment.
It is **protection.**

You are not waiting on God.
God has been waiting on your **alignment.**

Discipline is Not Restriction — It is Identity in Motion

Discipline is not about:

- Forcing yourself
- Punishing yourself
- Denying yourself
- Living in lack

Discipline is:

- **Consistency with your future in mind.**
- **Choosing long-term peace over short-term relief.**
- **Honoring the version of you you're becoming.**

Discipline says:

"I refuse to betray my future for temporary comfort."

Discipline is the daily *proof* that you believe in your future.

The Builder's Discipline Framework

There are three key disciplines required to sustain wealth:

Discipline	Purpose	Identity Statement
Consistency	Keeps you grounded	"I show up even when I don't feel like it."
Clarity	Keeps you focused	"I know where I'm going and why."
Accountability	Keeps you aligned	"I do not build alone."

Discipline is not something you find.
It is something you **build through repetition.**

The Daily Builder's Alignment Practice (15 Minutes a Day)

This practice rewires your identity through small, repeated alignment:

1. Look at Your Balances (No Emotion, Just Awareness)
This removes avoidance, anxiety, and guilt.

2. Make One Financial Decision That Honors Your Future

- Skip the impulse buy
- Transfer $5 to savings
- Pay $10 on debt
- Plan tomorrow's spending

3. Speak Your Identity Declaration Out Loud
(Because the mind obeys the voice.)

"I honor my future in the decisions I make today."

That's it.
Not overwhelming.
Not complicated.

Just **consistent alignment** with who you're becoming.

Identity changes through **repetition, not pressure.**

The Reason Most People Fail Is Not Lack of Information — It Is Lack of Rhythm

Even the best financial plan collapses without rhythm.

You don't need more motivation.
You need **momentum.**

Momentum comes from:

- Doing small things daily
- Remaining in your assignment lane
- Avoiding comparison
- Staying faithful when progress feels slow

Remember:
Seeds grow underground before anyone sees the garden.

Your discipline is the watering.
Your consistency is the sunlight.
Your patience is the soil.

And in due season — you will see the harvest.

Identity Declaration

I am disciplined.
I am consistent.
I choose long-term growth over temporary relief.
I am committed to my future and the legacy I am building.
I do not sabotage my increase.
I honor what I am becoming with the choices I make today.

Chapter Ten: Faith, Persistence & Delayed Gratification

How to Hold Steady While Your Future Grows

There will be a season where the work is visible only to you and God.
Where your effort is consistent, but the results appear slow.
Where your habits are changing, but your bank account hasn't caught up yet.
Where your identity is growing, but your environment hasn't shifted fully.

This is not failure.
This is **formation.**

Every breakthrough has a **hidden season**, where roots are being strengthened before the fruit appears.

God grows you *before* He grows what belongs to you.

Persistence is not about grinding harder —
Persistence is about **staying aligned long enough for the harvest to manifest.**

Faith Is Not Passive — It Is Active Agreement with Your Future

Faith is not simply believing that God *can*.
Faith is aligning your behavior as if God *already has*.

Faith says:

- *"I budget now like increase is on the way."*
- *"I save now because my future is worth preparing for."*
- *"I steward what I have as if more is coming."*

Faith is not waiting.
Faith is **building in expectation.**

Delayed Gratification Is Not Denial — It Is Direction

Delayed gratification is not:

- Punishment
- Restriction
- Suffering
- Lack

It is **focus.**
It is choosing your *future self* over your *current impulse.*

It is saying:

"I am worth strategic patience."

When you delay pleasure, you do not lose joy —
You **protect joy** so it arrives at the right time and in the right season.

The Emotional Side of Waiting (This Is Where Most Quit)

Waiting is not difficult because of time.
Waiting is difficult because of **comparison** and **doubt.**

- We compare our process to others' highlight reels.
- We fear "maybe this won't work."
- We get tired of being consistent without applause.
- We question our timing, our ability, our identity.

But hear this:

The enemy's only real strategy is to convince you to stop.

Because the moment you stop, everything freezes — the growth, the momentum, the alignment, the identity formation.

Persistence is spiritual warfare.
Staying consistent is deliverance in motion.

The Builder's Endurance Framework

To stay steady, you need three levels of support:

Support	Source	Purpose
Spiritual Strength	Prayer, worship, scripture	Keeps the heart aligned
Emotional Strength	Reflection, journaling, community	Keeps the mind grounded
Practical Strength	Systems, routines, money appointment	Keeps your life in alignment

When your **spirit, emotions, and habits** agree —
you become **unshakeable.**

Daily Endurance Practice (10 Minutes)

1. Speak Your Identity Out Loud
Your voice tells your mind what is true.

2. Review Your Why
Why are you building?
Who are you breaking cycles for?
Whose story changes because you stayed?

3. Take One Financial Step Forward
Not ten steps.
Just one.
Every day.

Momentum > Motivation.

Signs You Are On the Right Track (Even If It Feels Slow)

- You are more intentional with spending.
- You check your finances with less anxiety.
- You say "not right now" with peace.
- You think before reacting.
- Your goals feel clearer.
- You are no longer overwhelmed by money conversations.

These are not small changes —
These are **identity shifts.**

Where identity goes…
income follows.

Identity Declaration

I will not rush my process.
I will not abandon my progress.
I am growing in wisdom, strength, and alignment every
single day.
I honor my future with patience and persistence.
My harvest will arrive in its appointed time.
And I will be ready when it comes.

Chapter Eleven: Breaking the Generational Ceiling

How to End the Cycle for Good

Some struggles don't start with you.
But they *can end with you.*

You are not just healing your finances—
you are breaking a generational pattern that has repeated for decades.

The way your family handled money…
The way they spoke about money…
The way they *feared, avoided,* or *survived* money…

All of it shaped the identity you began life with.

But identity is not inheritance.
Identity is **chosen.**

And this is the moment you choose differently.

What You Inherited Was a Pattern, Not a Destiny

Your family did not fail.
They **did the best they could** with the understanding they had.

They survived seasons you may never know.
They stretched miracles out of moments that didn't make

sense.

They made a way when there was no way.

Honor them.

But don't repeat what broke them.

They gave you:

- Strength
- Resilience
- Faith
- Grit
- Endurance
- Resourcefulness

These are the materials required to build wealth.

You just needed the **identity and structure to direct them.**

The Generational Ceiling

A generational ceiling is the highest level of financial, emotional, or identity stability that your family system has reached so far.

Your parents went as far as *they* could.
Now the ceiling becomes your floor.

You are not starting from lack.
You are starting from legacy.

Even if the legacy was strength in struggle.

Breaking the Cycle Requires Three Shifts

Area	Old Pattern	New Identity Shift
Mindset	"We survive."	"We build."
Language	"We can't afford it."	"How can we create it?"
Behavior	Reacting to life.	Structuring life.

Cycles break not through intensity,
but through **consistent, identity-aligned choices.**

Your Family Needs You to Go First

Not because they were wrong—
But because they **did not have access to what you have now:**

- Information
- Insight
- Identity work
- Stewardship strategy
- Emotional and spiritual healing
- Awareness of patterns

You are the *first* to see the pattern clearly.
That is not a burden.
That is **a calling.**

Your healing is your lineage's turning point.

How to Lead Your Household into Financial Identity Shift?

1. Model, Don't Force

People don't change because you tell them to.
They change because they *witness the fruit of your alignment.*

2. Communicate in Peace

Replace financial blame conversations with:

- Vision
- Future planning
- Shared goals

3. Introduce Rhythms, Not Rules

Rhythms feel safe.
Rules feel controlling.

4. Teach Through Testimony

"What God is doing in me" > "Here's what you need to do."

Generational Leadership Looks Like:

- Saying **no** when the family used to say **yes**
- Saving when the family used to spend to cope
- Setting boundaries where chaos used to live
- Making plans where survival used to govern
- Speaking peace into places where panic was normal

This is not rebellion.
This is **restoration.**

You are rebuilding the family's relationship with:

- Money
- Self-worth
- Identity
- Legacy
- Faith

This Is Who You Are Now

You are the breaker of cycles.
You are the restorer of order.
You are the one who turns survival into strategy.
You are the one who transforms lack into legacy.
You are the one who will be remembered for rerouting the bloodline.

Your family's story changes because *you said yes.*

Identity Declaration

I honor those who came before me by breaking the patterns they could not see.
I carry the strength of my lineage, and I build new systems of wisdom, peace, and abundance.
The cycle ends with me.
The legacy begins with me.
And generations after me will live in the overflow of the identity I am choosing today.

SECTION IV: Walking Out

Your New Identity

Chapter Twelve: Living in Overflow

How to Maintain Peace, Purpose, and Identity When Increase Arrives

There comes a moment where the breakthrough is no longer a prayer request — it is your reality.

Where:

- The bills are paid on time.
- The savings account grows.
- Income increases.
- Opportunities appear.
- Your mind is steady.
- Your emotions are calm.
- Your decisions are intentional.
- Peace becomes your normal.

And it is here — in this new place — that many people experience a surprising fear:

"What if I lose what I've gained?"

But hear this clearly:

Overflow is not fragile when it is built on identity.
Money becomes unstable only when identity is unstable.

You did not arrive here by accident.
You came here through:

- Healing
- Alignment
- Structure

- Discipline
- Purpose
- Consistency
- Faith

What God has built in you cannot be undone by circumstance.

You are not lucky.
You are aligned.

Overflow Is Not About Having More — It Is About *Becoming More*

Overflow is:

- Mental clarity
- Emotional stability
- Spiritual grounding
- Purpose-driven stewardship
- Confidence in calling
- Calm decision-making
- Financial rhythm that supports peace

Overflow is not a number.
Overflow is an **identity state.**

You don't just *have* overflow.
You are overflow.

Walking in Overflow Requires Three Core Commitments

Commitment	Description	Identity Message
1. Protect Your Peace	Remove chaos, confusion, and rushed decisions	"My peace is sacred."
2. Maintain Your Rhythms	Keep your weekly money appointment and structure	"I honor what I've built."
3. Steward Expansion Intentionally	Don't grow faster than your identity can sustain	"I build with wisdom, not impulse."

Increase reveals character.
Overflow reveals maturity.

And you have become **mature enough to hold more.**

Do Not Shrink to Make Others Comfortable

When you step into overflow:

- Some people will misunderstand you.
- Some will project their insecurities.
- Some will expect you to stay where they are.
- Some will say you've changed.

And you have.

Because **healing changes identity.**
Wisdom changes identity.

Stewardship changes identity.
Purpose changes identity.

You are not obligated to apologize for your growth.

Do not dim your light to fit a room that no longer reflects your calling.

Leadership requires visibility.
Legacy requires courage.
Destiny requires elevation.

Walk tall.

Overflow Has a Purpose Bigger Than You

Your abundance is not only for:

- Comfort
- Ease
- Enjoyment

It is also for:

- Assignment
- Impact
- Legacy
- Provision
- Generational healing
- Kingdom advancement

God is trusting you not only to **receive** abundance —

but to **reassign** it.

You are becoming:

- The lender.
- The founder.
- The supporter.
- The sponsor.
- The generational repairer.
- The one who funds the vision God placed in your heart.

This is **your era of stewardship and authority.**

Identity Declaration

I walk in overflow with confidence.
I am not afraid of abundance.
I am trusted to steward increase wisely.
I do not shrink, I do not apologize, I do not doubt.
The grace on my life makes room for overflow.
I live in alignment, peace, and purpose.
I am the standard-setter, the legacy-bearer, the cycle-breaker.
And I walk in victory every day.

Chapter Thirteen: The New Financial Identity

The Final Shift and Your Ongoing Journey

There comes a moment where a person is no longer
becoming — they have **become.**

Where the shift is not something they are *working toward* —
It is something they *walk in.*

Where the old identity:

- Loses its voice
- Loses its influence
- Loses its authority

And the new identity:

- Speaks louder
- Stands stronger
- Lives fully

This is that moment.

The shift is no longer a lesson.
The shift is **you.**

The Old Identity Has No Permission Here

The identity that:

- Spent to cope
- Feared money conversations
- Played small
- Chased approval
- Lived in survival
- Felt unworthy of overflow

That identity has been **dismantled.**
Its agreements have been broken.
Its power has been revoked.

You are no longer reacting to your past.
You are responding to your calling.

You are not escaping cycles.
You are establishing legacy.

You are not trying to become a builder.
You are a builder.

Your New Identity Speaks with Authority

You think differently now.
You move differently now.
You see yourself differently now.

You have learned:

- How to steward peace
- How to align with purpose
- How to build financial capacity
- How to create increase from assignment
- How to maintain consistency
- How to wait without quitting
- How to lead your lineage forward

This is not motivation.
This is **formation.**

This Identity Must Be Lived, Not Remembered

Your financial identity is not something you visit occasionally.
It is something you **embody daily.**

To maintain this identity:

- Keep your weekly money appointment.
- Make decisions from the future you are building.
- Protect your peace like it is treasure — because it is.
- Continue building one aligned step at a time.
- Surround yourself with voices that **feed growth**, not survival.
- Speak your identity even when it feels quiet.
- Rest when needed.
- Rise when called.

This is your **ongoing spiritual, emotional, and financial rhythm.**

Your Life Is Now a Testimony of Transformation

Your story will:

- Encourage those who feel stuck
- Inspire those who are afraid to start
- Affirm those who are healing
- Lead those who are ready to build
- Restore those who lost hope

You will look back and say:

"That was the moment everything changed."

Not because of income.
Not because of opportunity.
Not because of timing.

But because **your identity changed.**

Once identity shifts, everything else *must* shift.

Life has no choice but to rearrange itself around who you
believe you are.

This Is Your Commissioning

Stand in your identity.
Walk in your calling.
Lead your family.
Honor your assignment.
Build with consistency.
Grow with grace.
Increase with wisdom.
Steward with excellence.
Love with fullness.
Give with joy.
Multiply with intention.
Rest with peace.
Believe with courage.

Your lineage will remember your name.

Because **you were the one** who broke the cycle…
And replaced it with legacy.

Final Identity Declaration

Speak this aloud — with strength, with ownership, with certainty:

I am the one God trusted to shift this generation.
I am healed, whole, wise, disciplined, and aligned.
I create, build, steward, and multiply with purpose.
Lack is no longer my identity.
Struggle is no longer my narrative.
Survival is no longer my story.
I walk in overflow, clarity, peace, and divine assignment.
I am the cycle breaker.
I am the legacy builder.
I am the financial identity shift.
And everything connected to me will prosper.

Amen.

Completing *The Financial Identity Shift* means you can no longer blame numbers for what was rooted in identity. The first step now is ownership. Decide that the version of you who operated from limitation is no longer in control. Write down the identity you are stepping into and define it clearly. What does this version of you believe about money? How does this version handle pressure, opportunity, and increase? Identity must be named before it can be embodied.

Next, audit your current financial behavior through the lens of your new identity. Do your spending habits reflect the person you are becoming? Does your savings strategy align with the future you envision? Restructure where necessary. Establish systems, automate savings, create a written wealth-building plan, and set clear short-term and long-term goals. Your identity shift must now produce structural alignment.

Then strengthen your environment and reinforce your growth daily. Surround yourself with individuals who think strategically and steward responsibly. Continue expanding your financial knowledge and exposure. Speak abundance, act with discipline, and make decisions rooted in purpose rather than impulse. The shift has occurred internally—now let your habits confirm it externally.

Other Books by Rev. Darryl Bass

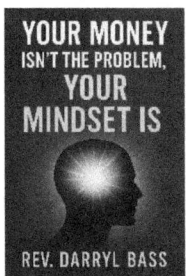

Your Money Isn't the Problem, Your Mindset Is

A transformational work that challenges limiting financial beliefs and redefines wealth from the inside out, empowering readers to align their identity with abundance and responsibility.

This Is Why You're Broke

A bold and unapologetic examination of the habits, beliefs, and financial behaviors that keep people trapped in cycles of struggle. This book confronts uncomfortable truths and replaces excuses with execution, helping readers shift from reactive spending to strategic wealth building.

Healing Your Financial Trauma

This book addresses the psychological and emotional roots of money struggles, helping readers break cycles, confront financial pain, and rebuild confidence and stability.

The Life Progression System

A comprehensive blueprint for intentional living, The Life Progression System guides readers through structured personal growth, goal alignment, mindset transformation, and legacy building. It equips individuals with practical tools to move from drifting through life to deliberately designing it.

The Life Progression System Workbook

A comprehensive blueprint for intentional living, The Life Progression System guides readers through structured personal growth, goal alignment, mindset transformation, and legacy building. It equips individuals with practical tools to move from drifting through life to deliberately designing it.

Financial Progression System

This book provides a step-by-step roadmap to financial stability and long-term wealth building. It teaches readers how to increase income, eliminate debt, build credit, create savings systems, and establish generational financial security.

Borrowed Futures

A wake-up call about the hidden costs of debt and financial shortcuts, showing readers how to escape debt cycles and build futures without financial bondage.

Life Insurance: The Gift of Life After Life

More than a policy explanation, this book reframes life insurance as a strategic wealth-building and legacy-protection tool. It educates families on how to use life insurance for income replacement, debt protection, estate planning, generational wealth transfer, and financial leverage.

The Intellectual Property Wealth Blueprint

A strategic guide to turning knowledge into income, this book teaches creators how to package ideas into books, courses, systems, and assets that generate scalable and recurring revenue streams.

The Intellectual Property Wealth Blueprint 2.0

Focused on licensing, certification, and legacy systems, this volume expands intellectual property into scalable enterprises that create long-term wealth and generational ownership structures.

The Overcomer's Wealth Plan

A resilient strategy guide for those rising from adversity, this book outlines disciplined financial recovery, structured planning, and long-term legacy development.

The Debt Eliminator

Coming 2026

What if 2026 was the year everything changed?

What if this was the year you stopped surviving... and started building?
The year you stopped juggling bills... and started creating wealth?
The year debt stopped controlling your decisions?

The **Debt Eliminator** is not another budgeting class.
It is a structured financial transformation system designed to help individuals and families break free from consumer debt, rebuild financial confidence, and establish a foundation for long-term wealth.

This course was built for hardworking people who are tired of living paycheck to paycheck. It was created for families who want stability, not stress. It was designed for individuals who know they are capable of more—but need a system that works.

What the Debt Eliminator Will Teach You:

• How to eliminate consumer debt strategically and aggressively
• How to increase income without adding overwhelm
• How to rebuild and optimize your credit profile
• How to build savings while eliminating debt
• How to structure emergency funds and protection plans
• How to shift your financial identity from borrower to builder
• How to create systems that prevent debt from returning

This is not theory.
This is execution.

Through step-by-step modules, implementation tools, accountability structure, and real-life application, you will learn how to take control of your money instead of letting it control you.

Imagine waking up without financial anxiety.
Imagine having a plan.
Imagine watching your balances decrease and your confidence increase.
Imagine positioning your household for ownership, investing, and generational legacy.

That transformation begins in 2026.

The Debt Eliminator is more than a course.
It is a movement toward financial clarity, discipline, and freedom.

Get ready to break cycles.
Get ready to build stability.
Get ready to eliminate debt—permanently.

The Debt Eliminator — Launching 2026.

Join our waiting list Today!
https://savingssolution.org/join

The Financial Freedom Revolution Tour

Launching 2026

This is not a seminar.
This is not a motivational rally.
This is a financial awakening.

The **Financial Freedom Revolution Tour** is a live, high-impact experience designed to ignite transformation in individuals, families, entrepreneurs, and communities ready to break financial cycles and build generational stability.

For too long, people have been working harder but falling further behind. Income rises. Expenses rise. Stress rises. Yet true financial progress feels out of reach.

The Revolution changes that.

This national tour brings together powerful teaching, real strategy, live coaching, and structured execution plans that move attendees from confusion to clarity—and from debt to disciplined wealth-building.

What You'll Experience:

- A clear roadmap to financial stability and long-term wealth
- Step-by-step strategies for eliminating consumer debt
- Income growth frameworks and entrepreneurship positioning
- Credit optimization and financial leverage strategies
- Protection planning and legacy-building principles
- Live financial assessments and actionable implementation

steps
• A mindset shift from survival thinking to ownership thinking

This is not inspiration without structure.
This is strategy with accountability.

The Financial Freedom Revolution Tour is built for families who want peace instead of pressure. For entrepreneurs who want profit with structure. For leaders who understand that financial stability is the foundation for community impact.

Imagine thousands gathered in one space—learning, planning, committing to real change.
Imagine leaving with a clear blueprint instead of just excitement.
Imagine knowing exactly what steps to take the next day.

This is more than an event.
It is a declaration that debt cycles end here.
It is a call to financial responsibility, ownership, and generational leadership.

Cities across the country will host this movement in 2026.

Seats will fill.
Lives will shift.
Legacies will be built.

The Financial Freedom Revolution Tour — Coming 2026.

This is the year you stop reacting to money
…and start commanding it.

The revolution begins with one decision.
https://savingssolution.org/tour

Follow on Social Media

Facebook

https://www.facebook.com/LPSCoach

Twitter

https://twitter.com/LPS_Coach

Instagram

https://www.instagram.com/lps_coach/

YouTube

https://www.youtube.com/@life_progression_
system

TikTok

https://www.tiktok.com/@debt_annihilator

LinkedIn

https://www.linkedin.com/in/lpscoach/

www.ingramcontent.com/pod-product-compliance
Lightning Source LLC
Chambersburg PA
CBHW071225220526
45468CB00002B/739